50 Ways to Make Up

Introduction

It happens to all of us at some point—a fight with our loved one. It might seem like you're fighting over something important, but when it's over, you just feel hollow and sick inside. What have you done? How can you make up? Will your lover ever forgive you?

The following suggestions are tried and true. Don't try the same one twice; your lover will catch on and begin to suspect that your attempts at forgiveness are not sincere!

1. Borrow a guitar, or a friend who plays the guitar, and serenade your lover with their favorite songs. For maximum effect, do this at their office, and make sure there are plenty of colleagues around to offer you moral support.

2. Give your lover a booklet of homemade coupons for ten services that you can perform. These should be for whatever will appeal most to your partner. (Do the laundry, make a home-cooked meal, give a backrub—use your imagination!)

3. Spray your lover's pillow with your perfume or cologne so that they will continue to think of you as they fall asleep at night.

4. Send your lover a favorite piece of lingerie—something he's seen you in before and that he will remember well.

5. When you talk to your lover after you've broken up, make sure you mention how much fun you're having dating other people. Try to date his or her friends as much as possible.

6. Arrange to meet your lover for lunch to talk about your breakup. Arrive at the restaurant wearing only a raincoat with nothing on underneath. If you can meet at a hotel restaurant, you'll probably be back together within the hour.

7. Stop by your lover's family's home on Christmas Eve. Bring a delicious apple pie and small gifts for everyone. Be especially nice to all the other relatives. After you leave, everyone will enjoin your lover for you two to get back together.

8. Make your lover a cassette tape that tells them all the things you'd like to do with them in bed when you get back together. You can also leave lots of sexy messages for your lover on their answering machine.

9. Win the lottery. Nothing fans old flames better than seeing your picture in the newspaper holding one of those gigantic checks.

10. If you hear that your lover is sick, make them a batch of this delicious chicken soup. Even if you're not a gourmet cook, you can handle the recipe. Stop by unexpectedly and serve it to your lover on a bed tray. It's sure to warm the cockles of their heart, and they'll wonder why they ever wanted to live without you. People feel especially vulnerable when they're sick, so be *very* nice and take full advantage of the situation to cast yourself in a new, sensitive, gentle light.

Lori's Favorite Chicken Soup

Ingredients:

4 chicken breast halves
3 or 4 carrots, chopped
4 stalks celery, chopped
2 large onions, cut into wedges
3 cloves garlic, smashed
5 whole cloves—not garlic cloves—dried whole
  cloves (the kind you stick on a ham!)
1 tablespoon dried basil
1 small bunch parsley, chopped
2 large cans chicken broth
salt and pepper to taste

In a large soup pot, place chicken and broth. Add enough water to cover chicken. Add the other ingredients and bring the mixture to a boil over medium heat. Turn heat down and simmer soup for 1½ hours, skimming off any fat that rises to the surface. When the soup is ready, remove the chicken from the bones, cut it into bite-size pieces, and return it to the soup. Add salt and pepper to soup, if desired. For chicken noodle soup, cook noodles separately and then add to the soup pot. This soup is guaranteed to make anyone feel better!

11. Show up at your lover's door with two airline tickets to an exotic destination. Whisk them away for a long, romantic weekend.

12. Take your lover out dancing. Get dressed up, bring your lover a corsage or a bouquet, and take them out to a romantic restaurant that has dance music. It will be hard for them to stay mad at you when you're dancing cheek to cheek (and hip to hip).

13. Keep in touch regularly with as many of your lover's relatives as possible. (Sisters are especially good for this purpose.) If they like you, they will work on your lover on your behalf. Pay special attention to grandmothers!

14. Set the scene for a romantic make-up dinner. Leave your office early and go home to cook your lover's favorite meal. Remember to put on the right music, light lots of candles, and chill a bottle of fine wine or champagne. Buy some bubble bath and put it next to the bathtub. Then slip into something more comfortable just before your lover arrives home.

15. Buy your lover an erotic book with directions for a variety of sexual adventures. Mark the ones that sound interesting to you, and ask your partner to tell you which of the suggestions they'd like to try. Take turns!

16. Send lots and lots of flowers. It's the old standard, but it almost always works.

17. Call your lover and tell them that you are planning to go on vacation to a gorgeous beach resort and you'd like their help. You've just bought some sexy bathing suits and you want them to help you choose which ones you should take with you.

18. Invite your lover out for Chinese food and slip an apology into the fortune cookie.

19. Take your lover to the beach. Hire a skywriter to fly overhead to write "I'm sorry."

20. Go on a long vacation and send lots of postcards. Tell your lover about all the fun things you're doing, but never say you miss them!

21. Get season tickets to your lover's favorite sporting event. Each week, let your lover know who you're taking with you. If you're feeling daring, you can also use these tickets to bribe your lover into a date.

22. Tell your lover all the new tricks you've learned since breaking up (and we don't mean card tricks, either). Do your homework (there are a lot of good books out there)—and be explicit.

23. Bring your lover a puppy and tell them that you want to raise it together.

24. Start showing up at your lover's favorite haunts with a new date each week. When you see your lover, make sure to introduce them to your date.

25. Write your lover a letter telling them that you're sorry that things are not good between you. Be the first one to take the blame for what went wrong. After you make up, there will be plenty of opportunities for you to blame them for other things!

26. Cry, howl, or scream until your lover finally gives in (or has you put away).

27. Tell your lover that you've met someone else who is very special, and that you think you might be falling in love. But you have some doubts about the new person, and you want your lover to meet you for a drink and to give you some advice.

28. Invite your lover over to watch *Last Tango in Paris*. Work on your French accent during the movie and then surprise your lover with airline tickets for a weekend in Paris.

29. Tell your lover that you'll be posing nude for a local art class, and invite them to look at some of the art. Arousing this kind of jealousy is always a good ploy.

30. Ask one of your friends to invite your lover to a party, to meet someone the friend thinks is perfect for your lover. But it's really only to be a party of two. When your lover arrives, work fast!

31. Threaten to expose your lover's innermost secrets unless they make up with you. Remember to keep that sweet smile on your face while you're threatening.

32. Once you've decided it's time to get back together, arrive on your lover's doorstep with some roses and a picnic basket containing a special dinner. Bring a blanket with you, and spend the evening with your lover on an indoor picnic. That blanket could come in very handy!

33. Hide small tokens of affection around your lover's apartment. Leave little love notes for them to find in unexpected places.

34. Surprise your lover on a Sunday morning by showing up with a hot breakfast and the newspaper. You may find you don't have a lot of time for reading! If you still have a key, let yourself in and bring the breakfast to your lover in bed. Don't forget to put a single rose on the tray.

35. Start doing all those little things around the house that your lover has been bugging you about for months. Sneak back in to clean out the closet, change those lightbulbs, weed the garden, paint the garage, etc. Soon they will realize that they don't want to live without you—or they will have to change the locks.

36. If all else fails, buy jewelry: any type of ring, anything with a heart—or better yet, anything with a diamond.

37. Take your lover with you to the scene of your first date. Tell them all the reasons you first fell in love with them. The déjà vu should work in your favor.

38. Bake your lover a heart-shaped chocolate cake and write an apology on the icing.

39. Slip a love note under your lover's door each day until they relent and make up with you.

40. Send your lover erotic e-mail messages so that they think of you all day long. Include references to all the favorite things you did together.

41. Have friends fix up your lover with all the losers they know at the office. You'll start looking better and better, and they will begin to desperately want you back.

42. Join your lover's gym and work out nearby, wearing very skimpy gym clothes to show off your physique. Flirt like mad with other people there.

43. Find out who your lover is interested in, and tell that person all the weird things that your lover did when you went out with them. Once your lover has been dumped by their new romantic interest, you'll suddenly begin to look a lot more appealing.

44. Spray-paint devotions of your undying love on the sidewalk in front of their house. You should be back together by the time it washes away.

45. Convince your lover to celebrate Valentine's Day on the fourteenth of every month—not just February!

46. Invite your lover to a friendly game of strip poker. Neglect to invite any other guests, and make sure you let your lover win.

47. Rent a motorcycle for a summer weekend and invite your lover to buzz around town with you.

48. Make a cassette of all the songs that mean something special to the two of you, and send it to your lover. Music always evokes strong memories, and the tape is sure to make your lover yearn for you again.

49. If all else fails, get on your knees and beg. Groveling is optional.

50. The only surefire way to make up: ask your lover to marry you.

50 Ways to
BREAK UP/
Make Up
with Your Lover

Lori Salkin and Rob Sperry

POCKET BOOKS
New York London Toronto Sydney Tokyo Singapore

POCKET BOOKS, a division of Simon & Schuster Inc.
1230 Avenue of the Americas, New York, NY 10020

ISBN: 0-671-00208-2

First Pocket Books hardcover printing February 1997

10 9 8 7 6 5 4 3 2 1

POCKET and colophon are registered trademarks of
Simon & Schuster Inc.

Printed in the U.S.A.

To all our former flames,
who inspired many of the ideas
in this book

The authors would like to thank their siblings, Laura (who always lets her opinions be known) and Michael (who keeps Lori's boyfriends in line).

Special thanks to Ling Lucas and Ed Vesneske, our literary agents. You are as wise as you are wacky.

We would also like to thank Amy Einhorn and everyone at Pocket Books for their vision and generosity.

INTRODUCTION

A relationship is like a yoyo: it has its ups and downs. Couples constantly go back and forth between breaking up and getting back together, sometimes for months, before finally deciding to either tie the knot or call it quits.

It's human nature to never know for sure what you really want. Let's face it: love is fickle. One minute you're showering together; the next night, he's sleeping on the couch. Sometimes you talk to each other five times a day; other times, you avoid her phone calls like the plague. Through all the ups and downs, it's important to keep your options open—just in case your lover wins the lottery.

Woody Allen once said that a relationship is like a shark: it has to keep moving or it will die. So whether you're breaking up or making up, you have to keep things moving (of course, you may not feel that

Woody Allen is the best source for advice on relation-ships).

This book is a source of inspiration for anyone who feels stuck in a relationship that's going nowhere—it's full of suggestions of how to break up *and* make up with your lover. You'll probably need both, so we've put them together in one neat package that you can turn to over and over and over again.

Good luck!

50 Ways to Break Up

Introduction

You know when it's time. The relationship is over, and you're ready to move on. But convincing your lover that it's time to hit the road isn't always easy. You need to be subtle—and a little devious. And you need to get away unscathed. What do you do?

The following suggestions offer something for everyone. All of them are certain to elicit the same response—your lover will begin to wonder what they ever saw in you.

1. Break up with your lover in a restaurant or some other very public place. That way, they won't be able to make too much of a scene. When making the reservations, ask if there is a back door—just in case you need to make a fast getaway.

2. Change your diet drastically. Eat lots of raw garlic, cooked cabbage, and baked beans. Your lover will want to head for the hills.

3. Tell her that you think she'd look a lot better if she lost a little weight. (Guaranteed results if used on Valentine's Day or on her birthday.)

4. Here's one of the oldest tricks in the book; it's been around so long because it's highly effective. If you're straight, convince your lover that you are gay (not that there's anything wrong with it). If you're gay, convince your lover that you are straight (not that there's anything wrong with it). In either case, ask a good friend to play your new lover. There is one problem with this strategy, however: it can really dampen your love life (unless you happen to play on both teams).

5. The beach is a good place to break up with someone. That way, if your lover begins to cry, the sound of the crashing surf will muffle most of their sobs. And, if you never want to see your lover again, you can fake your own drowning.

6. If you're a man, tell her that you can't get married as long as your mother is alive. She'll walk immediately.

7. If you're a woman whose lover seems unwilling to make a more permanent commitment, try leaving several bridal magazines around your home. Tell him that you can't wait to have his baby. He should be inspired to make a fast getaway.

8. Tell your lover that you're allergic to their perfume, their hair, their body odor, their pet.

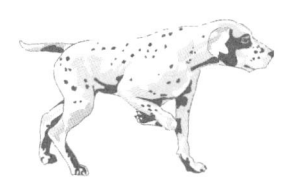

9. Let your lover know that you plan to be married by the Reverend Sun Myung Moon, in a ceremony of thousands.

10. Explain that you are going to quit working as soon as you get married, and that you expect your spouse to fully support you and your twenty adopted cats.

11. Tell your lover that it's always been your dream to live in a nudist colony. If they think this is a great idea, casually suggest that so much body hair might be considered unattractive to others.

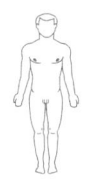

12. Ask him to dress up as a woman before you make love. If he likes this idea, *run away*. You now have a legitimate excuse to dump him.

13. Share stories with your lover about the terrifying types of psychotic illnesses that run in your family tree. Offer to take your partner to see your aunt Bertha, who resides at the local psychiatric prison ward.

14. Subscribe to several disgusting pornographic magazines. Leave these lying in plain view around your bed, and stare at them when you are making love. (Be careful, though, because when your partner's gone, you might start flipping through them on the nights when you're all alone.)

15. Tell him you don't love him anymore because he's losing his hair. Be certain you want to break up before trying this one; it's not an easy thing to forget or forgive.

16. Start writing to prisoners in the state penitentiary, and when you receive a reply, leave the letter out where your lover can see it. When he or she asks you about it, sheepishly explain that you are an ex-con.

17. Tell your lover you want to start having kids—right away. And that you'll want to have at least eight of them to help milk the cows you plan to graze in the back yard.

18. Leave a box of rat poison in plain view in the kitchen. If your lover asks you about it, tell him or her that it's time to kill the rat. And then mention something about needing more space.

19. Gain a lot of weight and lie around the house in your oldest and smelliest underwear (for some men, this is pretty normal). Tell your lover how nice it is now that you no longer need to impress him or her.

20. Buy a vibrator and leave it on top of the TV, where he is certain to see it while searching for the elusive remote control.

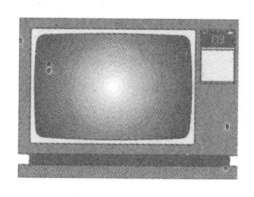

21. Tell her you'd like to try a ménage à trois. If she thinks this is a good idea, you have a decision to make. But remember, these sorts of relationships are not of the most stable variety.

22. Tell him you really want to sleep with his best friend. Or his boss. Or his iguana.

23. Talk to your lover constantly about your previous girlfriend or boyfriend, and remember to list all their good qualities. Wonder aloud what they might be doing now. . . .

24. Have a friend call you when your lover is visiting and take your call in another room. Act a little guilty, speak in a stage whisper, and tell your friend that you'll have to call back later because your mother is there.

25. If you're a woman, stop shaving all your body hair.

26. If you're a man, stop showering on weekends—and don't bother to wash your hair until Monday morning.

27. Stop wearing deodorant, even when you're planning to visit the gym. Make all your dates for immediately after working out.

28. Complain to your lover about his or her performance in bed. Start using a stopwatch, egg timer, or a miniature hourglass.

29. Buy yourself a large boa constrictor or a big hairy spider. Put its terrarium (complete with heat lamp) next to her side of the bed.

30. Tell your lover that what you like best about them is the fact that they didn't have that plastic surgery. Go on to say how brave they are.

31. Suggest breast or penile implants.

XXX

32. Ask your lover if they were better in bed when they were younger, or if they've always been this way.

33. Change the locks on your doors and get an unlisted phone number.

34. Start insisting that you want to make love only in the closet with the lights off.

35. Call your lover the wrong name on a regular basis. If you use the name of a previous girlfriend or boyfriend, so much the better. It works best if you say it in the heat of passion.

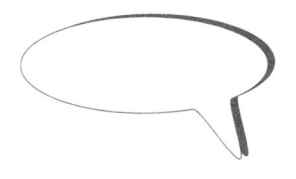

36. Flirt with waiters, waitresses, flight attendants, UPS deliverymen, and anyone else you come into contact with when you are with your lover.

37. Arrange to have someone call you in the middle of the night. Have your lover answer, and then instruct your friend to hang up when he or she picks up. Repeat as necessary until breakup occurs (usually from one to two weeks).

38. Start charging a lot of presents for yourself on your lover's credit cards (just write down the numbers the next time you go through his wallet or her purse). When your lover gets the charge statement, admit that they are your charges, but that as far as you're concerned, shopping is a lot less expensive than therapy.

39. Send a stripper to your lover's office on the day of their salary review. This is certain to humiliate your lover in front of their co-workers, but it will also put plenty of doubt into their mind about what their boss is thinking. Good or bad review, they'll come home a wreck.

40. Tell your lover that you really just want to be friends.

41. Mia Farrow allegedly sent Woody Allen a valentine that had been ripped apart by knives. Needless to say, it worked for her. We believe this type of threatening valentine might be effective for you, too.

42. Get a tattoo that says Mom.

43. Try to convince your lover that you have recently discovered that you are the one, true Messiah. Explain to him or her that this gives you the opportunity—no, the duty—to take numerous husbands or wives.

44. Start chewing tobacco. Spitting can be very unattractive—especially for a woman.

45. Stockpile weapons and ammunition in your home. Explain to your lover that you're preparing for the coming apocalypse.

46. Tell your lover that you're afraid you can't be there through thick and thin—only if they stay thin.

47. Start smoking a cigar in the car on the way home from work.

48. Start wearing a nose ring.

49. Tell your lover you'd like to move back in with your parents for a while to save some money.

50. Tell your lover you have a headache—each and every night. You'll be single soon enough.